LPs & Singles

John Miles Longden

821.914

MUDFOG

writing from teesside

Middlesbrough 1995

First published 1995 by
MUDFOG
c/o 11 Limes Road
Linthorpe
Middlesbrough
TS5

ISBN 1 899503 10 2

Acknowledgements

We would like to acknowledge the financial support
for this book from Northern Arts, and to thank all
those involved in Paranoia Press for work on the
manuscript over several years. Particular thanks should
go to Kate More, without whose determination it's
doubtful this collection would have appeared. Special
thanks also to Jerry Slater.

This selection of poems has been made by Andy Croft,
Pauline Plummer and Mark Robinson, with editorial
assistance from Linda Innes.

MUDFOG gratefully acknowledges the financial support of
Northern Arts and Middlesbrough Borough Council, and the
assistance of the Cleveland Arts Literature Development Unit.

MUDFOG is an independent publisher promoting the best new
writing from the Tees. For a full list of **MUDFOG** publications
write to **MUDFOG**, c/o 11 Limes Road, Linthorpe,
Middlesbrough, TS5.

Contents

Introduction

For the last twenty years of his life the long-haired, bearded portly figure of John Miles Longden was a familiar sight in Middlesbrough's cafés and pubs, where he ran a nomadic, unofficial 'University of Cleveland', holding informal seminars in a booming, roaring voice on any and every subject - Japanese verse forms, the history of Number Theory, George Bernard Shaw's phonetic alphabet, wild flowers, African literature, astronomy, Shakespeare's sonnets...

John was one of Teesside's best-loved eccentrics. He was also a formidable intellectual who enlarged the lives of several generations of writers in the North East. When he died in 1993, he left more than 5000 poems, mostly untyped, almost all of them unpublished. This book represents only a very small selection of an extraordinary body of poetry written over half a century, an introduction to the work of a remarkable man.

John Longden was born on 30 March 1921 in London. His father worked in the Civil Service, and his grandfather was an accountant in George V's royal household (as his great-grandfather had once been employed in Queen Victoria's). John liked to think he could remember standing as a very small child on a balcony at Buckingham Palace all dressed up in a little sailor suit, waving to the crowds below.

When John was ten the family moved to Middlesbrough and a large house on Thornfield Road, Linthorpe. He was educated at the Friend's School in Great Ayton, and then at Middlesbrough High School (where he was editor of the school magazine, secretary of the chess club and secretary of the Literary and Philosophical Society). In 1939 he won a scholarship to study PPE (Politics, Philosophy and

Economics) at New College, Oxford. There he found himself drawn into the political excitements of those years, secretary of the Cole Group and editor of the Labour Club weekly paper from 1940 to 1941. In 1940 he joined the Communist Party, to which he remained committed until its dissolution in 1991.

During the war he served in the Signals in India and Burma and engaged in famine-relief work on the Ganges delta. After the war he was employed as a Statistician, first in the ministry of Fuel and Power, and then at the Medical Research Council. In 1948 he was elected a Fellow of the Royal Statistical Sociey. Between 1950 and 1956 he worked as a statistician in Lagos, Nigeria, reurning to Britain to work as a research assistant at Cambridge. In 1962 he was appointed Professor of Applied Economics and Statistics at University College, Haile Selassi University, Addis Ababa. Other overseas academic appointments followed - at the University of Witwatersrand and the University of Adelaide, before in 1967 he returned to the North East to work as Senior Research Assistant at Newcastle University.

It was a distinguished academic career, and yet John was prevented from achieving the success that others expected of him because of desperate ill-health. Suffering from malaria in India 1943, he was treated with a prohibited synthetic anti-malarial drug, as a result of which he suffered a series of manic-depressive breakdowns. Returning to Teesside in 1968, his last paid employment was as a part-time glassman in the Talbot Cellar Bar in Stockton.

Although John almost married twice, it was in the early seventies that he met the great love of his life, a disabled ex-hairdresser with a drink problem. Michael Richmond's

8

impact on John may be gauged by 'Lucifer', a sequence of 269 sonnets written for Michael (Lucifer was John's nickname for Michael, the fallen angel). It was during this period that John found a new way of writing, influenced by Michael's strong local accent and his phonetic spelling, and he began re-writing much of his earlier poetry in a kind of generic Northern English. Unfortunately however, Michael's health and once bright spirit were failing. The combination of depression, deafness, drink and increasing paralysis proved unendurable, and after several attempts he succeeded in taking his own life in 1981.

John now devoted himself to painting and writing poetry, and to the single-handed development of a local literary culture. A great encourager of younger poets, John was immensely generous with his encyclopedic knowledge and - although he was always broke - with his heavily annotated library. In the late 1960s he ran anarchic poetry readings in the Purple Onion Café on Bottomley Street (later knocked down to make way for the Cleveland Centre); he was heavily involved in Pavilion Poets in Thornaby in the early 1970s; in the late 1970s, when punk was lean and mean, John was the oldest - and roundest - punk poet in town, complete with chains and safety pins; in the early 1980s he was runing poetry readings at the Dovecot Theatre in Stockton, encouraging young poets in the Middlesbrough branch of the Communist Party and helping to establish Teesside Writers Workshop.

Out of TWW came the magazine *Outlet*, and out of *Outlet* came the idea for a literary festival, so in the late 1980s John helped to organise the first *Writearound*, Cleveland's annual community writing festival, whose distinctive logo he designed. *Writearound* was to be a focus for much of the creative energy that John had helped to unblock, and he was always sure that *Writearound* should be different, a radical, democratic celebration with a strong sense of place. Its continued success owes a great deal to John's inspiration and to his insistence on its commitment to new and amateur local writers.

As the Teesside literary scene began to flourish, at last, he turned to his own poetry. He began to contribute to local publications - *Lazy Tees, Teesside Writers Workshop, Outlet, Tees Valley Writer* - and in 1990 he won the *Writearound* long poem competition. Eventually John was persuaded by friends to collect his poems for publication. *LPs and Singles* (i.e. long poems and short poems) was to have been his first book of poems.

John's own 'Sleeve Notes' help to explain some of his ideas about language and literature which inform the poems. What may look at first like wilfully eccentric spelling is simply an attempt to catch the rhythm and music of ordinary speech. Writing in a synthetic Northern vernacular was for John a way of resisting the mandarin English he detested. The poems are not as difficult as they look; just read the poems aloud, in an easy, conversational voice and you will hear John's own voice speaking. Some of the poems experiment with the shape of the words on the page, others are written in traditional and classical verse forms. The result is an idiosyncratic and intensely lyrical poetry of love, landscape and loss, a remarkable collection by one of the North East's most remarkable poets.

LPs & Singles was originally to have been published by Paranoia Press; unfortunately Paranoia folded in 1994. Mudfog was launched later that year to carry on the work of a small press that had done so much to help kick-start

Teesside's writing scene. While Mudfog's main aim is to publish small pamphlets of poetry and short-stories by Teesside writers, we hope to publish at least one full-length book a year. We are proud to begin with *LPs & Singles.*

Andy Croft

Sleeve Notes

Poetic forms help me harness 'n discipline the impulse to write, and encourage conciseness. With practice they get to be second nature.

Classical forms attract me, particularly the Sonnet, the Japanese Haiku, Tanka 'n Renga and the Elegaics of Antiquity. Our language is terse, 'n ten English syllables are roughly tantamount to the Japanese Haiku/Senryu's seventeen, or the Elegaic hexameter.

As the forms became natural, these resemblances suggested the idea of using Haiku and Tanka as verse-forms, and in due course combining them into what I call the Trivet (Tripod) of seven Tankas, equivalent to seven Elegaic Couplets, or one Sonnet - a blend of three classical poetic forms from three cultures and periods.

The reader will recognise the forms in these poems.

The poems are written conversationally, in the spoken voice. Few are declamatory. The intention is not to advise, but to appeal to the reader's outlook and experience, and let them adapt my text to their sentiments, and wrap my words in their sympathies. Some readers find it helpful to read the poems aloud or, preferably, imagine themselves doing so. As Sir Philip Sidney might have said, Look in your heart and read.

Aiming as I have done at a colloquial tone, I have preferred a Northern English style, by which I mean roughly that of Britain north of Brum. This reflects the development of our language beyond the limits of the latinized mandarin and computerized cosmopolitan of received standard royal Britspeak which denatures our

13

tongue.

To a degree I proffer a foretaste of the continuing evolution of English - terse, elliptic, and free of the redundant letter H. This style offers a reminder of the richness of colloquial and Northern speech, and reinforces the conversational tone.

As T.S. Eliot reminded us, speech must be the basic form of language. Writing and print are derivative 'n subsidiary, and lack the rich resources, the musicality of speech. It was in the centuries that English was unwritten that it became the unique instrument of a unique culture, and latterly the world's chief international language. This is the language we are bound to serve.

J.M.L

Octave

the worlds wet wounds lets out their crimson tide
the earth is feverish er flesh is scarred
scabbed maimed 'n poxed er arteries grow ard
'n lemming man achieves is suicide

o for a red death like a butchers bride
featureless tongueless eyeless limbless marred
in war 'n then to lie in state bestarred
'n belted wi' earths universal pride

then all me flesh made light shall day 'n night
pulse through me veins in alternatin skies
maelstroms 'a pearl poisoned wi' splendid dyes
convulsin times space girded citadels

blast to eternity the 7 hells
red
      flame
          gold
              green
                  lazuli
                      purple
                          white ::

*Poona Army Hospital. February 1944. Sonnet written
during a breakdown caused by wrong treatment for
malaria in Bengal.*

Sonnets For Two Voices

This sonnet sequence in pastiche was written for two
close friends between 1947 and 1951, in my later
twenties. They were married with a young daughter,
and were considering whether to have a second child.
Eventually they did. The father was a poet and senior
English master.

I. Mercantilism
- Michael Drayton -

Let's not debase the excellence of love
      that mixed with easier metal will not shine
      nor let the swift corrupting canker prove
      how soon false currency drives out the fine
The alchymists with grave and pleasant wit
      dreamed of a solvent nothing might endure
      more than a bubble roasted on a spit
      so perisheth all love that is unsure
Could tears and traffick pay the price love asketh
      mere wealth and works might fee us into heaven
      what bankrupt hearts this banker visage masketh
      cheap gratitude is bought but love is given
and doting parents recognise too late
their barren coupling in their children's hate ::

II. Antipodes
- William Shakespeare -

when the parched harvest yields a load of chaff
      soon blown away and little for the mill
      when every milestone seems an epitaph
      each hill the foothill to another hill
when the red indian summer burns away
      and makes a bonfire of our touchwood ease
      when leaves in tumbled libraries decay
      shed from the empty bindings of the trees
when from the warm companionable beach
      the tides of winter excommunicate
      and barren loves desire can barely reach
      the cinder sunset dying in the grate
yet at your touch is the globe reversed
and this new summer fairer than the first ::

III. Commonwealth
- John Donne -

Wee beinge old shalle see owre Sunne lesse hotte
      Owre Themmes Icelanded Traffique at a Stay
      Owre Monarchie ungratefulle or forgotte
      Owre inke-blakke Curles and Charcole Sonnettes
          grey
All privie Treasure robbes owre privie Peace
      Feares bought lyke Janizzaries rewle the State
      Owre Eden Wildernesse and profitlesse
      Thieves on owre Gallows Thornes to crown
          owre Gates
Sarpentes and Tares threw all owre Garden reigne
      Owre Flockes lyke Abells slayne by Husbandrie
      Since owre Bestowinge onlie is owre Gaine
      Onlie owre Seede is owre Prosperitie
And as the Globe turnes rounde owre Island sees
Hir Commonwealth's at hir Antipodes ::

IV. Bereavement
- John Milton -

All amorous pow'rs are to the dark resign'd
      Which we toward in tender duty bound
      Have travailed now ten years Nor have we found
      That we can part with undivided mind
Our ways before us but our wealth behind
      As Orpheus daring Hades dusk profound
      His rescued bride unseen could yet confound
      All with one backward glance If we have pined
In such brief absences what shall sustain
      The one whom our last parting leaves alone
      What link propitious cheer the hopeless gloom?
Unless our issue prove such sorrow vain
      And by their vertue justifie our own
      All we have common builds our common tomb ::

V. Sorrow
- Wm Wordsworth -

Sorrow thy tutelage seems hard to bear
      though wisely hazarded we harbour still
      the private burden of an obstinate will
      absolved unworthily of wonted care
Because neglect of duty does not spare
      even the worthiest of our loves to kill
      sorrow that goes no deeper can fulfill
      only the empty office of despair
Must I miscall thee Folly's punishment
      seeking an easy answer Do we spend
      Youths riches only to see Age lament
      all past desires? Rather I call thee friend
whose searching kindness teaches in the end
that what we grieved at first we least repent ::

VI. Heretics
- John Keats -

when I see men vowed to idolatries
      zealots for fame or sovranty or gold
      their lives the graveyards of their victories
      and all their disenchanted altars cold
when I see those who down the years have come
      alone and friendless to a shadowy age
      like mariners who bring great cargoes home
      and landing find themselves no anchorage
then I renounce the folly of appeal
      finding them set upon their flotsam fate
      and most devoutly in our love I feel
      the kindly summers richly fortunate
and hoarded griefs dissolving pity none
but childless lovers and their unborn son ::

VII. Nativity
- G.M.Hopkins -

maid-mated mother mastering mankindness tongue-rough-
    tender
    in Passovers passion fruitful great since harvest-
    hearted October
    thanksgives she Gods good-shepherding
Mary :   Though lamblate born in December
    blessed be the Babe that sucks my breastmilk sleeps
    sweet on my shoulder
    starbright in heaven-hosted darkness delivered in
    Bethlehem
    goldgifted frankincense-fine He Godfathered I
    Godchilded
    Blessedest I among women surest tomorrow of
    shelter
    Be promise of peace His lullaby peaceproud His
    principality

Joseph : Tha'll not be cradled coldly careclosed and father-
    fostered
    with all that craft can bestow or kindred kindness
    endeavour
    Would I were worldlier-wiser had more than wood-
    wit to offer
    more than olive and oak and the fall-felled forest to
    master -

Blessed the Babe but bitterly   prince indeed of the Passover
the carpenters nails in his hands   His birthright the beam on
    his shoulder ::

1947-51

Nightfall

To Michael

The Love god rules us all -
let us too yield to the love god
Virgil : Eclogue X, 69

First Leaf - Cabbage

Guz London Norwich
        'n Cambridge 'n now back north
                to the big 'ouse
fm 2 interviews
        visits to two friends 'n one
                reechoin
reverberatin
        night 'n aa must lull the gong
                the um the ush
our friends flow through us
        their familiarity
                breeds contentment
seasons of wrappers
        off of magazines unread
                'n set aside
bareback manilla
        nibblin the nibless ballpoint
                tickles me and

Second Leaf - Frost Fern

is me art shortin
>   voltages jolt 'n rattle
>>   the box a' words
over the cocked roof
>   over Michaels low attic
>>   a shootin star
sun in a snowflake
>   dazzles the midnight zenith
>>   'n fades as ash
dusty days later
>   on the crisp cold calender
>>   f'm nights afore
as out a' season
>   out a' the black 'n blue west
>>   love continues
'n the key is 'ere
>   between street 'n stair below
>>   the open door

Third Leaf - Strawberry

Aad given you up -
    the foal in bed currycombs
        is mane fidgets
Ow does yer like it -
    the room moves into focus
        ranged on the bed
skin beneath a quilt
    air beneath feathers the dog
        beneath the skin
the old blue bigot
    Loves Awakening two fires
        the record player
'n TV jumble
    yesterdies gear tomorrows
        nex years sometimes
'n theres no pier glass
    objects 'n pictures serve as
        purblind mirrors

Fourth Leaf - Fig

dead centre Michael
     enthroned with dog in the bed
         against stair rails
looks at me sketches
     wants us to draw im some time
         skims some poems
awkward in the quilt
     Michael flaunts is modesty
         listens 'n asks
as we trade our lives
     over pauses to renew
         records or pee
on 'is conditions
     aa shames im clear a' the quilt
         aa undresses
as e maks coffees
     aa sprawls along the green couch
         below the bed

Fifth Leaf - Olive

discussin coffees
    both black Mock-modest Michael
        black yer'd be fab -
Wy - Why is because
    Colour burns in the darkness
        stars in the sky -
Would yer like to ave
    the dogs place - yes indeed - locks
        abet luvvers
early aa slip up
    the latch soon circumspection
        informs on me
'n now on Michael
    as the double bed confines
        its prisoners
two to share a cell
    'n abed 'n a body
        'n ours 'n ours

Sixth Leaf - Vine

the crash 'n grapple
      a' torrents the stutterin
            of riveters
nothin a' that no
      power is over asels
            over the flow
a' arm into arm
      into arm thigh into thigh
            mouth into mouth
doin one biddin
      as 30 years melt away
            'n we're brothers
electric twilight
      noon remembers the low room
            a bar too warm
the roar a' the fan
      cut 'n the dog on the couch
            the quilt again

Seventh Leaf - Maidenhair

Turn out the light
      turn on the twilight 'n mak love -
           quotin mesel
coilin uncoilin
      Michael visits the 3 lamps
           turns us both black
then f'ra moment
      the draught in our arms shivers
           in the square bed
'n we're that famished
      munchin shouldermeat breastmeat
           'n knucklebones
me studded watchstrap
      purrs round is shoulderblades
           is air crackles
wi' stars in the night
      we turns f'm chamber music
           to nestin chairs

Eighth Leaf - Poppy

the wind breathes through us
       lulls us through a spell a' sleep
             back to the sun
Good morning - Michael
       turns t' me voice 'n me arms
             are the socket
blind 'n dumb we say
       grace for each other 'n feel
             asels awake
wi' chains a' kisses
       Michael crashes the curtains
             explodes the day
Sorry no coffee -
       e taks first turn to go down
             Can y' draw me -
time for the life class
       aa rout out paper a stool
             charcoal 'n pens

Ninth Leaf - Bamboo

a mop 'n a grin
      lounges over gibbon arms
          'n boneyard legs
'n against all odds
      the scaffold a' spillikins
          recomposes
crane pylon mantis
      hieroglyph ideogram
          out a' Euclid
a dish a' lips
      a wobble a' nose 'n to spare
          'n two eyes of grey
lose the artsease face
      blowin breakfast under the
          smoke of 'is air
aa itch to draw
      only the web of angles
          gawk 'n gangle

Tenth leaf - Skeleton

Michael breasts the quilt
      after Cocteau curls in a cage
            sprawls out knee-igh
3 poses bam
      back to bed till a 'orn toots
            Sundy service
a race into jeans
      navy jersey 'n sneakers
            down 'n away
'n Michael leaves us
      to copy the 3 sketches
            collect me kit
like it carn appen
      overnight to a write off
            bumpin 50
put back on the road
      for the spin of a lifetime
            Michael makes me

Eleventh Leaf - Apple

ow ad aa written
     Love the stone in the snowball
        were ad aa been
not in the service
     of 'is desires nor mine not
        in the blessin
'n consecration
     of cathedrals for pigeons
        mountains for mice
nor the nurturin
     a' sons 'n daughters a' more
        surplus beauty
merely though all these
     nor new friends but the sharp proof
        that love is youth
a artbeat off out
     a' memory 'n lease'olds
        our real estate

Twelfth Leaf - Lime

a tricorn crackles
    in me palm 'n on paper
        drawn limeleaf size
veins curl in the crust
    varicose out a' the leaf
        ribs coil 'n crack
this leaf is me own
    aa find it 'n aa own it
        now as its dead
green on the lime tree
    it owns asel aa dozen
        aa carn own life
barrin me own life
    easy to lose 'n forget
        'n ard to live
in a single night
    will there be others Michael
        you show us this ::

1970

US

My battledress
has thigh pockets
for wound dressings
as & when

And now a sharp
crease runs through them
as they hang on
the moonlit armchair

In the moonlight
I also see
a wound that cuts
into your groin

Let me staunch it
with the dressing
that lies ready
on my thigh ::

1973

Oppos
- epigram -

poppy red jungle ats 'n ripened torsos
shuttlin 'n rallyin through calls 'n pauses
over the way a neighbour 'n is lad
plays toyshop tennis in there small backyard
carn see the lad the fence between us dwindles
me field   theres is dads image in the windows ::

1977

Dayspring

RIDING
across
snug Northallerton's
lonely stile
Richmond
'n Richmondshire eye
the 'Ambledons

Cleveland's
Roseberry sees tides
come 'n go
wrinklin
a oily ocean
The Norse Sea

frownin
f'm a musselled beach
'n sheer bluff
to Witby
abbey 'n 'arbour
sand 'n jet

COLDMOOR
winter
'olds out on the tops
'n the poles
summer
launches glaciers
as icebergs

driftin
wakes a' wite puff through
the cold aisles
the fall
sets keen claws scalpin
pole 'n peak

wite snows
wite chrysanthemums
shrouds 'n days
allus
new year's snow buries
last year's drifts

WHITBY
'oarfrost
black trees blossomin
as we sleep
shadders
moultin wite feathers
curdled rain

boxin
this rainbow igloo
bleak 'n wite
watter
levellin wi' the 'ills
'n the sky

snowstorms
blast immaculate
dunes 'n dells
snowmen
bandages a' snow
'n a' grass

COLD POOL BECK
snowdrops
carn shoot through iron-
ice no way
snowploughin
arsy-verse routes through
cobbled cars

yellow
AA's run wite tigers
in their tanks
collies
shepherd flocks a' gulls
off the lake

flamethrowers
fireaters knockin back
sunbeams
brickbats
in snowballs clutches
a' scotch eggs

SNOW HALL

summer
dies 'ard 'n winter
dies 'arder
a slab
a' ice roofs the lake
shore t' shore

darkness
dusts th' earth wi' frost
draws it up
flagstones
embroidered wi' glass
filigree

sprinklins
crumbs or sugar or
table salt
ruins
a' snowman charrin
on the turf

SUNNYCROSS

Michael
moves f'm 'is fireside
to 'is pitcher-
window
tradin 'eat f' light
dusk f' day

sunlight
dimples 'is grey gloom
chafes 'is cheeks
today
snatchin tomorrers
'appiness

snowdrops
stretchin wi' the days
peal out a
quiet
carillon grasses
dare t' grow

SLEEPY HOLLOW

the sap
stirs late 'appen spring's
in no 'urry
larnin
t' live on the light
wi' the leaves

the grass
'n butterflies still
winterbound
flies'll
fetch fish wen the ice
giz over

a break
gleamin through the cloud
arfer dusk
yesdy
early abed today
slow to stir

STEPPING STONES

dark days
telescopin to
twilit nights
florists
offerin daffydills
at 'arf price

chessmen
mate in the town 'all
last weekend
2 birds
dude 'n drab wi' wite
wing-flashes

glean chaff
off of the numb grass
the deep freeze
redbreast
carols 'is 'art out
f'm 'is post

LOW LANE
mebbe
wen tha works it out
'tint that bad
missin
the short cut to the
bookmakers

layin
low through dull days 'n
sad seasons
sleepin
wiles the sun's bumpin
past the turn

dallyin
in the wild goose chase
a' the spring
screamin
a month late into
a small world

BELLEVUE
mornin
smokes dawn   damp bonfires
into mist
tissue
wrappin thas present
f'm thas view

iron
trees suckle there buds
yawn into life
worn walls
let on there's jazz in
them old bricks

postmen
lift there brown polls f'm
their brown bags
seein
gay poster-colours
on our doors

HOB HOLE

silver
streaks ribbonin over
the rubber
bands they
shuck yesterday 'n
a big thrush

trainin
a peckish pecker 'n
a keen eye
rovin
in search of a meal
'n a mate

a 'ouseproud
lad's off to 'Ob 'Ole
f' brownstone
boulders
to fortify 'is
raw rockery

RICHMOND
gold rings
git asels mislaid
in the dumps
thas folks
'n frens still grabs tha
'n 'olds fast

like tha
sets thas own price on
thas assets
rubber
checks don't worry none
watch em bounce

gimme
tha 'and 'n tha 'art gimme
like aa done
promise
thas allus me only
Valentine ::

1979

Hypochondria

all me life
    this top specialist
        treats us free

e's the authority
    I'm is patient like

sorts us out
    regler e's the best
        keeps us well

right round the zodiac
    while me ticker ticks

'Arley Street's
    tall boys carn touch im
        nice wi' it too

e'll nivver stint nowt
    yeah yeah its is pleasure

Mum 'n Dad
    as there clinics too
        'n the kids

you bet aa maks sure
    our lass as the same

on the Nash
    not free enterprise
        beat that cock

yeah the pooch as it
    so do the spiders

wotsisname
        wy Dr. Boddy
             mind evvyone
on earth as there own
      learned Boddies too ::

1983

Cage
Elegiacs

steel erects its tents
calls clamps a' navvies
calls priests nuns poliss
church infirmary schools

ony a church angs out
a century on but
cold rusts rent the shops
in gaps plugs the igh street

lost terraces bares
shards 'n bun pennies
brick flats fence this pub
wi' plywood winderpanes

drawin our idle 'ands
their bargain bitters ::

1983

Tent

grey eiderdown
     slashed wi' azure stiff legs
                        a' light
feel for the skyline
     till we eclipse the sun

as we turn
     towards the starry 'osts
                our backs
to our own star day strikes
     the circus marquee

all day through
     the skys one way glass
              the stars
eye our world we return
     their distant quizzin -

through glass eyes
     tubes a' virgin steel
              ridin
starstruck roundabouts
     we outspy all the heavens

'n dissect
     their elements weighin
             the wirlin
waltzes a' dead stars
     we live in their past

cold stars shine
        on their coroners
                        lost graves
here all time coincides
                in the mind a' man

the cosmos
        commemorates mans
                        brashness
'n its yokefellow
                magnanimity ::

1987

Heirloom/Trace

3 insects
    climb a crack across
            leagues a' cliff
Omar's telescope
            identifies them
We see us
    us the day before
            yesterday
Mao's eyes sting to rework
            the creased precipice
cramped backs
            'n thighs reenactin
                11 hours
on a ledge a earthquake
            snapped across a rock
sheer luck
    that ancient iccup
            serves our turn
this first Xmastide
            our past's our present
forbears
    dreamed a' granchildren
            we embody
Orions promises
            luvs light chain armour
by our feet
            3 ants bustle along
                a pale line
spannin a boulder
            they're goin our way see
magic
    isn't magical
            the way insight is
the world carn overcrowd
            the arts 'n minds a' men ::

1987

Ducdame

(As You Like It, ii 5)

Ducdame - Wills word calls fools into a ring -
               brings taxis in a trice - revives flat beer -
               sets up a penny market in hot air
               foregathering to agree to disagree -
               builds roundabouts -
               graphs grids a' one way signs -

Ducdame - sells Tupperware & keeps in touch
               sneaks long shots a' the Royles -
               keeps pop groups goin -
               won't turn the telly off nor ride by bus -
               lays in on pollin days 'n slags the pols -
               carn stand wind
                        cold
                              rain
                                    snow
                                    nor nowt like that -

               ankers for Peter Pan 'n joins the army =

Ducdames a spell to keep things as they are ::

1984

Now

now it urts
        urts to be awake
                urts to be
Athens the marble
        citys burnin now

like wood
        tinder bracken
                ancient peat
the fire down belows
                burnin underground

Julys
        the eat buildin up
                towards August
the all or nothin month
                corn on the campfires

widowers
        thrown on the pyres
                a' young eroes
joinin their lost gods
                sunsets through smoke

urts the eyes
        like the worst a' griefs
                growin to see
the dead don't need our tears
                we're mournin asels

they exit
        they crack like light bulbs
                'n its dark
our lights die by inches
                a grief at a time

artless
     'n andsome they
          leave us a world
a' pieties duties
          reluctantly done

Michael
     5 years ago 'n
          Andy now
aa swims
     out to sea
          wi mist in me eyes ::

1987

Retread

Part I Casing

Well yer raw 'ere
were me tale's stale bait
                Jean's jacked
in spinnin it now
though a' course its Jeans yarn

I'm an erk
'n ground crew are not
                medics
still aa'll 'ave a stab
wiles Jeans set the tea

Race pigeons
or nudge planes 'n aa
                does both
the Isles are 'andy enough
to me Harrogate home

Stornaway offers
me a berth Aa meets Jean
                These days
they let midwives wed
before they retire

Seein folk safe
into the world or down
                the sky
onto the tarmac
we've lives on our 'ands

Truly we're all
our cousins' keepers

like Cain
Each landin each birth
yer catchin yer breath

Wiles all's well
'n yer can come back
to life
Yer own life's briefly
yours in trust once more

The Atlantic's
chained f'm Unst to Islay
by islands
Our Budgie circles
Lewis   Britain's biggest

We're leanin
in parkin orbit
Jeanie
points   Look   They're chivvyin
the ewes off the runway -

Too true they are
'N aa's come ere to Air
Traffic
Control   Come to work wi'
collies as colleagues

Me seatmate
points again   She says
Stornaway's
all go - Aa see all go 'ere means
a easy goin lifestyle

Jeans local
she does us the honours

       for the Isles
the cliffs a' gannets
the light young artists

      carn paint nor
credit the stacked seas
        the peace
crofters 'angs on to
by their fingernails

     The Outer Isles
'undreds a ageless rocks
        a gneiss
twelve lived on bitten
like a poems margins

     Lewis means the Isle
wi' lochs by the 'undred
        Stornaways
the main town the airport
the air aa monitors

     Callanish's
stone circle 40
      centuries
to the west monitors
the maverick moon

    'oos 4 week
'andshakes travesty
     the way a brace
a' islanders lingers
over a encounter

    massagin
the Gaelic into

the flesh
fingerin the feelins
their tongues are tenderin

The islanders
except in Stornaway
          tells yer
Wen God made time 'E
made all 'E wanted

Wot's the rush -
Here throwouts tak their time
          to rot
In front a' one black house
2 write-offs rust away

in Ardnoils
wite dunes some bullocks
          nosed out
Norse ivory chessmen
8 centuries old

We are still guests
seasoned guests yet guests
          Sea birds
outnumber the folk
umpteen thousandfold

Fish 'n sheep
cast as many votes
          as us
Their wealth maintains us
on these rocky groynes

Midges drive
troops back 'ome frantic

'n off
the firin ranges
the loch-pocked highlands

The heroes' bawls
reecho drown the shells
the torps
Flexed fossils defend
lost 'oards a' Uzbeck gold

Harris's hard
rock denies graveroom
on the east
The dead 'as to go west
to enlist a sexton

A jeweller
shy Ewan McLeod   sells us
our rings
James McLeod rents us
is empty cottage

'N we know
the unbelievable's
spot on
like cockerels crowin
long afore the dawn

Part II Retread

Jean needs us
Needs us now aa's as good
as nuked
plastered all over
a truck's barred muzzle

The wite Mini
a write-off flung down
both lanes
Ambulance men f'm
Stornaway peelin me off

Aa'm bluddy
shattered   Palatic
Cat's meat
Life-support systems
buttressin the 'ulk

Sisters 'n
families 'n surgeons
'olds their
breath for me last gasp
Someone sticks out but

'n summat
responds Jean needs me
that much
'n me like mutton
a plastered dummy

Tubes drips pumps
plumbin does duty
for offals

Dials meters echoes
intensive nurses

    calibrate
their apparatus
        agog
for quavers off-key
off-tone off-tempo

    They envelop
they cocoon an adult
       infant
all but entombed 'n
unbearably unborn

    'N somethin
some smudge some scrapin
      a' life
keeps demurrin aa aint
a terminal case

    Un 'opeful
spectacled medics
       skiddin
on black ice clutch at
'andsets 'n joysticks

    at death's door
for the extras maybe
      Stabilised
for the young midwife
for Jeanie me 'elpmate

    Willin me
fiercely 'artlessly
      to luv

batterin me back
to a wary awareness a' life

Me eye peekin
into a world outside
me skin
The chrysalis cracks
ajar   Aa goggles

tunnel-eyed
Their raw red babes see
far more
than aa sees then   Me eye
swims in a lost world

the untuned screen
on a mugged telly
Senseless
aa confronts feelins
'Artbeats outpace me arts

'N soon Well
nex month   aa asts Sister
Oo am aa -
They know 'n aa know as
aa recknise faces

Like Sister's
me Mums 'n me Dad's
or so
Nurse tells me   One face seems
less Jeanie's than me own

Me enemy's
within 'atin me as
'aa am like

grabbin the life as
aa lacks 'n loathes so

Aa's drownin
Lemme drown   A 'arf lifes
better
'n resurrection
Lay off 'n let me be

Wild 'awsers
winch me wreck 2 ways   Can
raw egg choose
to be 'atched or 'ard boiled
coddled or beaten

Aa 'olds pop mags
upsy-downsy   Same
difference
All Jean does is nag
nag nag nag nag nag

Now me 'ands work
me Parker pen's gone
on strike
Me wingspread's still gooseflesh
isn't this nex door

Doors are blind
Back door plays cupboard
the layout's
daft as algebra
They fret about me

They say aa act   strange
but to me it's all strange
'n aa's fine

'N aa manage things
aa can lay me 'ands on

Jeanie 'ounds me
Drat the woman she won't let
me sleep
Just a bit a' kip
Aa'll be right as rain

There's no one round
is like 'er   Noone else
badgers
me dawn to nightlight
These Are Yer In-Laws

Josephine
& Hugh & Valerie -
Vee. A. Ell
Val - Three   Times   Tables
& Three   Threes Is Nine -

Tie Yer Laces -
No neatly - Dee. O. Gee. Is
Dog - Neil's
En. E. I. Ell. - & Jay. E. A. EnI. E. I's
No   Not Gin - Jeanie -

Back at work
aa josh the blokes 'n
sup teas
then doss down for 2 hours
'n kip after lunch

Carn control
me own carcase nivver
mind planes

so aa 'andle the baggage
'n lug the in-flight meals

    Buttin yer 'ed
agin prison walls
        it's like
All me check-ups charm
the specialists not us

    We ram crags
'arder 'n 'arder
        across
a treeless tundra
Skye 'angs a long way off yet

    Nursery school
Infants   Junior   High
        Jeans druv
me so far   The firm
giz us day release

    to regrind
me previous degree
        Aa's not
mesel aa's ony
the facsimile

    recycled
son usband neighbour
        A actor
playin me role parrot-
fashion believin

    as Jeanie 'n
evvybody does
      aa'm me

Threaded nerve by nerve
braincell by braincell

on the warp
of a dogsbody in
coma
Lewis' light Jeanie's luv
'er sturdy impatience

A madman
gunned down Leonardo's
cartoon
in shreds they're spendin
some years to restore

The Virgin
St Anne the 2 bairns
reemerge
to match the images
cameras bequeath

'n the faith
our restorers share
that film
'n lenses can serve
patients faithfully

Aa'm restored
yet aa'm no the lad
as lost
is rag two three four
times a day at ome

And at work
Aa's bin through death's door
'N lived

6 year this side a' it
since Jeanie switched trades

    f'm midwife
to therapist 'n raised
              'er dead
man f'm pale porridge
to a 'uman a someone

    rallyin me wi'
the rueful ruthless
              mania
a' luv the strange face
of an alien self

    Jeanie 'n me were
in luv before   aa
              fancy
Now we luv   Now we are one
enmeshed past teasin

    Out into
shreds 'n chips 'n cells
              a suet
We're spliced into a 'awser
Us one mind one flesh

    committed
by our past to serve
              one life
The price we pay is wot
the job's worth innit

    Jeanie'll not
agree At least not to

me face
Yer larns yer inmost
secrets second-'and

Aas 'er child
made in 'er image
a' me
the image a' self-luv
'er foto-album like

a statue
vexed to life the fruit
a' incest
as we all are aa guess
underneath the skin

Din't aa spark
Jeanie into flame
between
courtin 'n coma
Aa's er   like she's me

Aas 'ugs er the way
aa 'ugs mesel now pleased
as punch
aa's sussed mesel out
'n peeled mesel off

the blind bull
in the china shop
a' exile
the self-deception
of a red serge cape

Let me be 'n

aa'll Kamikaze
                again
This gold ring should be in
me snout aa reckons

        Jeanie luv
dinna fash yersel
                nae mair
Thas stots oop a stob
to block tha's passage

        Call us 'ome
n aa'll come poundin
                stay mum
aa'll blockade tha's doors
to bar tha's way out

        Aa nuzzles
Jeans 'ands there's no pail
                no churn
The nex manger's blank
We're missin summat

        Me midwife
'oo better knows as
                'er bairns
is other people's
& other people

        The genie's
outa' the bottle
                for keeps
but it's not empty
so Jean charms the dregs

No No chance
Nivver in this world
                aa'd not
a' reckoned on it
'N now aa know it like

        the impossible's
down thc road a piece
                some sit
'n sit on their 'ands
on the yellowin verge

        believin
they carn believe in
                nothin
They carn see a future
as steers the present

        On this card
a star guides wise men
                to a birth
Yesterday's godchild
'n tomorrow's god

Part III Ikon

You're midwives
'n you're both Polish
      Aa's eard
'ow after the last war
they revived Warsaw

as it was
but brand new   Jerry'd
      smashed it
You fotolithoed
Warsaw stone for stone

F'm the old plans
'n the old master-drawins
      grew ageless
baroque boulevards
virgin Gothic fanes

Aa'd be thrilled
to explore the new Warsaw
      mesel
'n feel its firm pulse
its art its fabric

'N greet it
comradely knowin it
      grabs me
Like aa's bin rebuilt
f'm the ruins as well

Aa imagine
you'll know 'ow it is
      wi' me

'ow ard to accept 'ow strange
that Neil now was Neil then

    Its dead 'ard
but now aa know noone knows
        asels
better than aa does
Aa'm dead lucky in luv ::

1988

Hour Glass

yer B i b l e's a toilet roll
yer Sun's a paperweight
yer sky's slug fodder
the P.M. a flea bite
Hitler's a yawn
time a wisp
all
a echo
of a sigh
a spark of life
the art's imagining
the form's a' perception
like yer self-image is God ::

1988

Mort Skelton

I. Punk

Sunburst keys
    on Skeltons festoon
        a' brass chain
    Nicked f'm the markets
    dungeon toilets next

the Old Town All
    Keys interrogate
        4 door cars
    'N larn beefy bikes
    to belt out Morts tune

till their tanks
    are wrung dry   'N their smashed
        hijacker
    drowns the kosher hogs
    down a old iron shaft

These fun bits
    crease a death-camp grin
        in the sheath
    a' sprayed cellulose
    on Mort's shaven skull

I'm into
    death Mort tells you It's
        me life's work -
    You ear is grin crackle
    like a squeezed popper

Death's me trip
    Aa mean its evvyone's
        Ennit mate
    Noone carn argue wi' that -
    Nor wi' is ugly smirk

darin yer
        to contradict im
                'n outface
        the 'orror video thug
        prudence 'olds at bay

II. Treat

Giz five quid
        Aa'll buy our last round
                        Professor -
        Is eyes swipe me 'and Me 'and's
        skulkin to me wallet

Yer cushy aa's
        in a good mood The eyes
                        menace me
        simulatin a int
        as e's not bluffin

But the bald
        appeal to me is to
                save 'is face
        Mondys e's allus skint
        is roll a few crumbs

For 4 days
        Mort keeps rangin bars
                for friends   Friends
        in need that is   Mates
        as 'e can cadge off

salvagin
        self-respect by not
                treatin back

                none a' us   E'd blush to
                treat mates reglar   E's

insulted
                wen me casual warmth
                        betrays me 'n
                the grim sympathy
                that tools our tandem

The kindly
                nostalgia of remote
                        brotherhood
wi' this balky brat
                panickin at life

III. Saints

Skelton's Mort
                to is intimates   but
                        a art student
                doin Creative Outrage
                to the authorities

This triff course
                is right up Mort's row
                        John Moores
                prized Morts *Leonardo*
                Paints the Last Picnic

onto is Red
                Customized Harley
                        Heritage
                on the Stonenge Run
                STARRIN Brando as Paul

Theyre all Hell's
      Angels   Jesus Xt
        'n St John
      are piebald lezzies
      Mort is St Judas

The Apostles
      scrabble fish 'n chips
        'n glug down
      their Newcastle Browns
      passin round the joints

Moores' Prize pays
      ony arf Morts fine for
        blasphemy
      E serves out the rest
      in clickety-clink

Does 2 months
      'n then some spoilsport
        meets is fine
      'n Mort nivver larns
      to break safes proply

IV. Wings

To 'im College
      stands for sacrilege
        in top gear
      Drugs Dirt Dredlocks Sex
      Mort's creative media

The 'atred e as
      for 'is spare body
        finds a vent
      in slashed vests tattoos
'andcuffs ammo-belts

Floral hose
        bloom through ripped denim
                jeans   unwashed
        since Mort dunked   issel
        in sump oil   just to win

a drugged bet
        a' one can a Lilt
                Then young Sue
        didn't pay up 'Er folks
        flitted to Torbay

She must pay up
        afore Mort'll wash
                the oily rags
        They're 'is bettin slip
        'is sense a' grievance

wi' the 'ole world
        Did 'e ast to be born
                a unwanted
        git as gits the blame
        wen mum 'n dad plays war

3 more brats
        get treated reglar
                Not Mort but
        till 'e runs away 'n shames
        'em into affection

E nivver
        forgives 'em for sayin
                We're sorry
        We'll make it up to yer -
        7 years too late

V. Blacks

Some summers
    'e 'elps 'is Uncle Clem
        'oo operates
    a funeral parlour
    at the end a' Westbourne Grove

Mort digs it
    Bearin wi' the square
        blue serge suit
    the patent Oxfords
    the black fabric gloves

'e upstages
    the departed dears
        the corpses
    flyin away wi' the fall-out
    a' smoke   Or inches down

into a raw 'ole
    Clods crumble on clods
        ashes dust
    ashes dusk to dusk
    The vibes are real cool

Back at Art
    College Mort's project
        is a punk-
    style funeral service
    Mort's Ell for Leather

His mutes bein
    skin-eds in one-piece
        black leathers
    84 eyelet
    black DM's Fingerless

black kid mitts
        Knuckle dusters wi'
                skulls   X-bones
        Shaved pates 'n no elmets
        so as to mark respect

VI. Oi

Bestridin
        wite Fifteen Undred
                class Kami-
        kazes to squire the 'earse
        The long flat artick

totes a black
        riderless Triumph
                The deceased
        in racin leathers
        throned on the pillion

Plus their box
        crammed wi' plastic flowers
                'N bottles
        to prime the punch-up
        Grief must not intrude

Nor good taste
        Nor priests lamentin
                the poor sods
they were introduced to
        via the coffin-lid

Billy Idol
        on tape snarls out The Will
                Lyrically
        The mutes make merry
        Theres no snivellin ghouls

Mort's Last Calls
    must ride triumphantly
        They're victors
    Ticker-tape heroes
    paraded through Rome

escorted
    by punks in their prime
        as handsome
    as the ham shindigs
    the deceased once shared

VII. Mates

Citizens
    'oo sowed wild oats 'n
        were as young
    as bony as fearful
    a' life as our Mort

Elf Levver
    was nivver launched   More's
        the pity
    Posthumous thinkin's
    wot they're fresh out of

Yet we envisage
    young Morts triumphal
        hit parade
    Morts shit 'its the fan
    for legions a' old mates

Mort's still way ahead
    'E olds is 'ands out
        and 'is art

to stiffs   cryin Cheerio -
Way down our branch line

zest flags off
        Morts late runnin train
                a' bravery
        on our way   Wiles we all stopped
        dead in our teen tracks

We 'arrowed 'ell
        We revived 'n rose
                Lived death down
        to joke about japes
        we were ashamed of once

Yet the high-flyer
        misses all the stops
                except the one
        the buffers evvyone
        overruns in the end

VIII. A Fair Cop

May aa 'ave a word Sir -
        A crewcut yuppie waves
                a bent badge
        'n aa carn quite place
        is familiar grin

Me plainclothes
        detective ushers
                me in the Wite Lion
        Shandy Professor -
        'n now aa suss the voice

Right Robbo
        shandy it is Yer off
                yer beat aa 'ope
        mate - The barman draws
        a 'appy-our double malt

Robbo adopts
        a dark nook a low
                tub table
It's this rhyme yer wrote
        The lads is worked up -

Nah not riled
        jealous like They carn
                twig 'oo is Mort
        'Arry says Count me out
        Aa weren't a art student

'N Baz says
        wen yer knew 'im e' weren't
                into bikes
        Chuck carn mind ever
        cadgin pints off yer

Choppers not
        inter funerals
                'specially
        not other people's
        They all flash alibis -

IX. Identikit

'N tak me Aa
    din't wear floral binks
            nor gungies
    Well We all wish we knew
    wich on us is Mort -

Drawin breath Rob
    tosses is double
           down the 'atch
    Nex is left pinky
    a gold ring's gleamin

Were's yer snaps
    Rob Bet yer burstin
           to show 'em round -
    Is wallets pregnant
    wi' wee Robbo's mugshots

Tell the lads
    Mort's noone special More
           a identikit
    of scraps 'n cuttins
    a' young warriors

Kids that's 'ad
    a 'ard time breakin free
           'atchin out
    at 'ome Makin Dad
    'n Mum Granpa 'n Gran

Mort's the verse
    on a greetins card
           sayin Act tough
    Yer folks is just folks
    fancy-dress ogres -

Yer right there
      Prof Werever they are
           cops nab em
      They buy our souls dirt cheap
      'n pay us not to grow up -

Robbo me arse
      bleeds for yer all the way
           to the Mint
      Yer cheeked bent bogies
      back at Sundy School ::

1989

Pass

An August Fridy
    Dusk is late tonight
Lads are playin football
    on a patch a' turf
Wen aa go out to watch for
    our small bat they're gone

On the mat nex day
    a arf sheet a' paper
Off a spiral-bound
    notebook Aa unfold
A note that drifts in
    'n out a' capitals

Were a boy as needs sex
    lists is bill a' fare
Look over yer gate
    Aa'll be out on the wall -
Aa looks front 'n back
    'n there's noone sat there

There isn't even
    a police cadet
Did e tap not knowin
    as aa's ard a' earin
Ave aa urt is feelins
    snubbed is loneliness

Listenin to the news
    blamed the knock on puss
E couldn't reach me
    'N now aa carn reach im
But aa tuck is note
    in me pension book ::

Spiders

to encourage
      self-elp in marooned
               spiders
      dangle a ladder
      down yer baths sheer walls
this forestalls
      the need to scoop em
               deftly
      f'm the bunkers slopes
      'n url em elsewhere
to mak lace
      werever they incline
               pillowin
      their silk macrame
      on evry surface
in evry
      orifice they find
               vacant
      nex to nothin feeds
      these hunger strikers ::
elp em out
      elp em elps asels
               likewise
      swimmins not their scene
      rubber ducks are ours
but spiders
      the poor souls uddle
               drownin
      in our ot water
      'n wettin agents
we saddle
      em wi' our own terror
               we cringe
      f'm their elplessness
'n scream at the deaf ::

                    1989

Shakescene

We were in Wells 'n playin at the Star Inn
Arry IV One Dick Burbage was took bad
wi' scrumpy fever   E let on e ad
a tertian ague   Will mustered a grin

Aa could play Falstaff like aa was is twin
We all roared Wiles the laugh was on the boys
Will toped stormed bluffed milked japes
                                'n growled Is voice
outranged Burbage's bear 'n rode the din

Yet camp 'n all e's Master Will turned Titan
the travesty rang true Is clownin' parodied
The Globes pet jackdaw as 'ad guarenteed
years a' packed houses 'n royal nights delightin

the nobs Our puppet master a' all arts
the man apart as wrote us all our parts ::

1989

7 Stars

Overtures - Horsehouses

I.
Encamped up Coverdale   we carn git aver
        the champagne skies wen we're   shot out at closin time
        Gropin down to the paddock   the last pint split and sunk
        we gape at the glitz a'   the Galaxy jewelry stall
We wake 'n worm our way onto the turf
        arf asleep The earthshine's   soft on the melon moon
        climbin the east 'n washin   the Milky Way into the west
        a wind-brushed bush bursts into   birdsong phrases
We sleep late

                Sunrise dawdles   like summer in The Dales
        wiles 6-Eyes' watch starts   twitterin at the tits

II.

We stir 'n stretch 'n   strain our pup-size tent
        Bemused beetles are busy on our ceilin
        We recapitulate   Tuesday plot the day
        two flip-flop bards wi' ballpoints runnin dry
'N recall the Merry   Morrismen seein off Yule
        stormin the needle North   magenta jitterbugs
        doin the cancan as   Clevelands ramparts loured
Planes buzz the Pole now 'n   rape 'n rack the watersheds
        they avalanche even the Alps   the Andes the Grampians
Orbspiders web the way we carn   winch through the tent-flaps

III.

Shoulderin the Coverdale sky a sycamore tests its strength
      Though e's six foot five inches   Six Eyes seems just a
          sucker though
      is eyes skim f'm skyline to skyline in a flash
We sup light a thousand lives old wi' a armpit Theakstons
      Say ow many lamb chops reach f'm Lichfield to the
          moon -
      One if it's large enough - Johnson turned the tables
Finger 'n thumb burn to the thrill a throwaway stardust
      The firmament we plumb's self-made we're zillionaires
      wi' minds as measure the megaverse we expand

IV.

Brotherly Cains   brand gods in their own image
      Thatchers boast thatched theodolites are best
      Writers go all out 'n utter the unthinkable
Wiles Dusty's just about bushed generally but 'e copes
      as best e can 'n plods down the promptest path in
         sight
      Mums feedbins that feast the foxes in turn
      clear eds 'n omnivores opt outa plastic plants
Nowt's often a real cool and   Wy nuke it Play it out
      Don't museums truffle the trailers for T-Rex movies
      Karl Marx's old cocoa tins   'n mediaeval mousetraps

V.

A burnt dale lies beyond the bone-dry boundary
     the Nidds three reservoirs dead dregs 'n brimstone sides
     Overhead a hawk hangs 'n watches
     us sup squash 'n sarnies by the butts
criss-cross Tornadoes strafe us deaf 'n bristlin
     three kingdom's defiled by indefensible defenders
F'm a ole in the scars   crawls a long worm a' water
     We trickle towards the cool treeline 'n the clay cliffs
     the bleachers a' pebbles   'n boulders round the twists
     'n saunter past a rustin chassis in the ashen shade

VI.

A flash-flood's felled a young ash   It fences the meadow
     a jury-rig water jump   in jade 'n brushed silver
     F'm the level trunk towers   a troop a tall offspring
     hung wi' bunches a green keys   bright birdfood 'n future
     ashlings
              Anywere Northallerton oversees
     nay anywhere in England the Norse ash is at home
     Burn green burn grey   graceful or sky-scourged
Odin's steed Yggdrasil rides the Ridings still

VII.

The River Cover wanders under the shadow
        a' alder 'n willow
                    Allegories jog ome
        down'ill down dale sculptin mixed-media
        landscapes a' legend   loneliness wrath 'n flux
        wild lyrics lookin for a lurk apart
        f'm alliteration   a life alive on thc tongue
        a mankind makkin emptiness enlightenin
        acceptance contentment nothingness satori
Doesn't Shakespeare mak Macbeth a bloke
        as crosses is conscience like we all of us do.

VIII.

Assassin traitor   mass murderer Macbeth
        comes closer than the next seat in the gods to
                ourselves
        'N we're the posterity e pines for   Our feelin
        For im is self-pity our silence soliloquy
Bonnie 'n Clyde   Lady Macbeth 'n Macbeth
        Gear that's the go   the glamour a' bein wanted
        Greed grabs a gat   Glory's a getaway in a hijacked V8
Fay 'n Warren are robbed they bring home no doorstop
                Oscars
        The double-take a the casts catastrophe grabs us
        we're the deft self-drivers dummies in gangster suits

IX.

Neether suit nor four weels mean nowt wen Dogpatch
  knows theyr'e there Noone carn wear em 'n carn fool
    em
  like a Harley Heritage wi' a empty elmet ung loose
  or a word-processor printin moon 'n June verse
The backs a' envelopes pastured Popes rhythmic lisp
  microscopes mak Newtons miniscripts legible
A portable stove packet soups well water
  serve to mak us a snack pendin a pub meal

X.

Our grass'll be green not gold wen we strike camp
  The lane to Leyburn labours as it winds
  We'll tak our time tak note a' edgerow weeds
  Vergin on witherin like one a' us is
Off to Ironopolis or on 'n on towards Herts
  roads roar the dark dazzles 'n smog smothers
  Coverdale's crammed onto compact discs
 Nostalgia's
  a memory label we must muster solo
Our Beowolves howl at our heels we leash em in
  'n mak for the hermitage
    Home is were bards belong ::

1990

7 Stars
The Toss

... lessenin ...
　　　... loosenin ...
　　　　　... listenin ...
　　　　　　　... listenin ...
　　... echoes ...
　　　... equals ...

thumb 'n finger	finger 'n thumb
around 'n	a round
space is	so small
fingers	carn feel i
in space three	spirits meet
three's a	thick throng
a crowd	in chaos
trinity's	tinnitus
two	tough
twin rogues rustlin	rakehells wrestlin
fight for	a fall
a foul	a failure
number three	referees
umpires	adjudge
tubs a' suet	Sumo wrestlers
blind	f'm birth
rough 'n sparky	rival spirits
know oo	they are
by the tricks	a' the trade
sleights 'n handholds	holds 'n breakfalls
the darks' dirty	dirty 'n draughty
thers no eyes to gouge out	in the game a' gods
a' gods	'n ghosts
till the fight	finishes

the fall guy's   first to bat
the topmost   taks the field
the bard tells   the tall tales

the scorer   allus scores
the accountant   the auditor
keep the books   bless the bride
The Holy   Hiptures
The Scrolly   Scriptures
the actuary   consecrates em
casts em   in concrete

the singers lyric   the lyre 'n the arp
the praiser   the poet
the singer's   a spirit

Alleluleia   Alleluleia
to the Laird   to the Lord
the piper   'n the purse
the teller   a' tales
blamelessly   shamelessly
'n loudly laudin   the Lairds larrikin

rent a muse hire a muse   here in the Highlands
Singer   For Sale
Bright Silver   'n Red Fame
The Money Value a'   I m m o r t a l i t y
Gifts   for Gifts
Potlatch   Plenty

A Bard   Brings
Great   Gifts
Fame   'n Shame
Disgrace   'n Glory
the blind ol beggarman   as us at is mercy
Skydish   'n Squarial
bring blackmailers   'n brigands to the box
the gift a tongues   The ghosts spokesman

Listenin	to silence
the dark blackenin	the drums flexin
The Big	Bang's Back
for Ziggys Next	Zillion Year Run

WalkupWalkup   WalkupWalkup
Laydees Kids Goddesses   Gods 'n Jemmun

W O W

Not theTruth the ole Truth   'n Nothin like the Truth
Oh No that's Box   Office Poison
we call   it just
A Jemmuns   Agreement
ShakeShake   SkinSkin

A n d

The Price You   Pay is Life
is Right is Wrong   is R i t u a l

Our Gods are silent .

.
.so They are eloquent ...

We are Their Voices .

.
.Our Gods speak for Us...

We speak for the Gods .

.
.Our voices are Theirs ....

Our voices are Theirs .

.
.We speak for Ourselves...

Listenin   Listenin ...
. . . Listen in

1990

Sunburst
- Life as Rhetoric -

We're almost 3 miles igh up the steeps a' Kilimanjaro
>A army a' forty-foot groundsel defends the peaks
>>dead rock
>'n in the tall flowerin crowns a' the giant lobelias
>that shelter under this forest a' vegetable pylons
>the Scarlet-Tufted Malachite Sunbirds shiver
>damp dejected 'n dumb in the equators dim dawn

Beyond Malindi across the wide-awake Indian Ocean
>way past Krakatoa Cotapaxi 'n yesterdays cinnabar
>>sundown
>over Lake Victoria 'n the Ruwenzori ranges
>STOP PRESS days nuclear bomb bursts big as a
>>million planets
>firin' the rage to live across the desert a' space
>as the dark continents spin out a' the earths own
>>shadow

All at once the summit seizes the sun f'm the air
>The snows ablaze Day skis down to the zone a'
>rubble-
>rock 'n tumbles 'n leaps 'n bounds to the treetops
>a' the skeletal forest Diamonds melt on the stalks
>'N now day dances anew to the music a' the melt
>a new day dances again to the music a' the melt

Zero The exhalted chorus rings Mount Kilimanjaro
>f'm every turret a' blossomin lobelia
>Birds blast defiance resume their territories
>'ardly pausin to breathe or to sip at the nectar
>>scarcely
>stirrin to fertilise their private chandeliers
>a' blossom were mute mates 'n chicks are grazin freely

Protected by their dads vaultin' canopy a' song
      'n the well-preened scarlet pennants a' is tufts
      the punchy confidence a' is arf-ounce display
      the family probe for honey wi' their biassed
          surgical beaks

Labourin up the volcano through the climates
      zone after zone - laden wi' all the traps
      as maks us masters a' Mollweides double
          dartboard
      'n the friends 'n foes a' all - our three naturalists
      clamber to glean all they can f'm nature's simple
          pattern
      sufficient unto the day until our arrival

They con this jewelled collar round Kilimanjaros peak
      script it 'n tape it 'n film it 'n put it on the air
      STARRIN The Scarlet-Tufted Long-Tailed
          Malachite Sunbird
      arf way to the 'eavens carollin for dear life
      Wife family 'n 3 scientists to support ::

1990

Teesside Twinned with the Universe

- A Sonnet for Wembley -

WOW as we breast the lip a' the long rise
      flanking the flatlands all along the Tees
      league upon league a' yellow crocuses
      embrace the dark flood-plain 'n fill our eyes
This swarm outshines our sister galaxies
      it fills the view the lungs the art the mind
      burstin f'm the black country a' the blind
      Here the entrenched osts a' Ironopolis
spread rape-gold vistas in the frozen night
      Gorse blooms invincible through all seasons
      a blaze then a few sparks Come rhyme come reason
      frost or flood drought or blizzard calm or riot
Clevelands gold lamps light up their massed barrage
Our twinned night sky's the Boro written large ::

1990

haiku

the windows weep all May 'n we watch 'em dry-eyed ::
shootin' stars our aim's dodgy but they fall ::
dusk curdles starlins drainin' f'm the sky ::
the balloon on a far lampost 3 a.m. moon ::
a deaf composer explorin' the unknown ::
listen the wind tells the tide the truth ::
one street lamp 'n a missel thrush singin' ::
a squirrel guards the empty bin f'm strollers ::
the road dips out a' sight into mind ::
a clear night the witch loses count a' the stars ::
a beige braid a' fatigue on the white gardenia ::
layin' pebbles back where the North Sea set them ::
the Arab boys watch Jordan renewin' a dead sea ::
two bats graze a street lamps halo till late ::

1992

Deepdale

I.

IN THE MALE LINE   Deepdales run back 'n back
way out a' sight past Lincoln 'n the Lakes
the settled look a' self-willed eldest sons
The distaff side's all Scots wi' Ayrshire farms
Auld Reekie   Aberdeen   'n Orkney crofts
drawn south to London's maelstrom 'n the sun

II.

THE FIRST page on the roll another John
Deepdale graces the Court a' George IV
wi' out disgrace John as is ed screwed on
all right   'n e unscrambles the 3 R's
turnin em to account as an accountant
a trade where there's small need for itchin palms

SO FOR A CENTURY we are Londoners
John's son John and is grandson Clifford also
accountants and Assistant Secretaries
to The Queen's Privy Purse their very self-
respect a mark of deference their man'ood
the obligation of invisible men

H.M. gives Harry Clifford the parcel-gilt
christenin mug   DJ and me drink out of
But aa've no son   the silver mug gets lent
to Mike 'n lifted Nowadays aa drink pints
not trinketfuls 'n as aa write aa taste
the dregs a' generations on me palate

III.

OVER THE BORDERS   We're three-quarters Scots
Two restless farmers turn their backs on wool
to thrive as aberdashers   Turn their backs
on Glasgow to thrive in St Paul's Church Yard
Both breed 'n breed   'n die afore their lads
are of age to shame their canny sires

FORBYE the salvage f'm their crash suffices
the orphans 'N the youngest a' the bairns'
Jessie's   own nest-egg enables er at twenty
seven to marry Clifford Deepdale bachelor
lately appointed to the lately married
Prince George their future King and Emperor

SO CLIFFORD is well fixed Once the two sons
D.J. and Winton grow their mother Jessie
finds interests a mind of er own non-violent
suffrage the Fabians   travel   elbow-room
After the War she signs no armistice
'Otels 'n lendin a 'and fill thirty years

D.J. goes off to Cromwell's public school
then Oxford The War grabs im   Mespot moves
im on to the Indian Army   Urdu 'n ponies
So Dad is well fixed too then jacks it in
'n sails 'ome to retrieve is parent's marriage
returns to Oxford claims a pass degree

IV.

THIS is a message in a bottle like
'n messages in bottles must be true
Which brings us to me mother's family
the Northern Isles were men all ply the sea

wile lasses raise the bairns 'n knit twin shrouds
appen a seaman ivver dies in bed

SAY Great Grandfather Bews the snow-capped Master
of a flyin tea-caddy a China clipper
a migrant bird ferryin arf the treasure
'a sunrise to is square Aberdeen hoose
F'm which is lass marries a young reluctant
lawyer a Mr Duncan and as issue

AUNT MARIE's four me mother two Consumption
steals their mother away   Their father finds
a housekeeper 'as a son 'n marries er
then kills asel soon after rather than
chew the cud a' Scots Law to raise is family
The grievin relict shrugs the orphans off

MARGARET JOSEPHINE me mother   nivver
forgives er father or forgets T.B.
Schoolgirl housemaid-cum-tutor student at
Mission 'n Armstrong Colleges landgirl clerk
wi' the air Force at Grantham then John Lewis's
Matron to all the residential staff

V.

AS LION LONDON roars f'm war to peace
Shaw's in the chair two andsome youngsters in
adjacent seats both look up to the sexy
sexagenarian 'n aa's a twinkle
under is juttin eyebrows as e smiles
The pair slip out together 'and in glove

BOTH bent before 'and on a boy to start with
to be named John   Their dreams 'n mine unite em
They register their vows Nine months to the night

the Zoo's beasts 'ear me cry across the way
Late snow marks the first time aa's shown outdoors
aa bronze all summer long parked in me pram

A GARDEN backs the ground-floor flat the fourth
nest that they occupy the first they settle
in a detatched part of Clapham in Wandsworth
furnished as best they can 'n walled wi' books
The post-war boom soon blows out Rheumatism
cripples me mother now Duncan's in er womb

VI.

A BLUE-EYED BABE wi' shoulders like the Downs
a lion's roar a flossy mane to match
a Bews to look at Like our parents favour
their firstborn they concur to indulge their second
in practice Guess aa should a' larned em better
bein the eldest but parents seldom learn

DAD is a quarter-miler built like a wippet
- tank a winged three-quarter in snowy stockins 'n
the Old Boys' side Summer Sundays we walk
Surrey wi' our vast pram Sometimes we all treat
the occupants a' London Zoo courtesy
a Ivory Ticket lent by Grandad's boss

YES yes yes Pantomimes Schneider planes
Peter Pan and is statue Veraswamy's
or Simpson's Surrey strolls Cake at B.P.
Street markets Privet-moth cocoons evolvin
in the soft 'umus under the south fence
Wakin to beaded webs that veil me view

VII.

ALL GOOD THINGS... Up North Dad finds a vocation
e trains in Lancashire We leapfrog over
to Cleveland there our brother David's born
Bonny 'n lusty at three months e dies
a cot death on the instant 'n me mother
withdraws into er garden 'n er pain

DAD REVS the Riding in is square black Essex
National Savings Committees tempt good people
to preach thrift they're the decent class of colleague
'e dovetails with Our 'ouse first 'oused a steelmaster
we bring the lost long back garden back to life
for yonx me mother taks no olidays

VIII.

SO DADS WELL FIXED for life until is Chairman
renounces the Ridings to tickle a banker pal
'n posts me old man to London Mother jibs
Dad applies to the new Assistance Board
a post as suits im 'n e nivver suits but
warm to the workers brimstone to is chiefs

IN 20 YEARS is duties drop 2 grades
or more is outlook dwindles Out a' time
e aims to cut is coat 'n taks me counsel
No go Laid off at 60 Dad blames Mother
for not appeasin bosses e pisses off
So atred is me parents' only bond

IX

LONG SINCE aa wins me way to Oxford thrillin
em both to bits Duncan goes south to dig
orticulture 'n the Navy 'n electrics
aa graduate to eavesdrop Shinto morse
We warp 'n weave the world   'n mak it ome
Duncan treats Mum to er one trip to Edinburgh

THERE we meet our Great-Gran a dozen cousins
we're only names 'n child'ood snapshots to
Dad makes it our last family reunion
War 'n two sons don't prop the partnership
come peace 'Olly 'n ivy mesh no more
Mother's a invalid Dad's on is own

MUM'S ORANGE JUICE tastes wrong The analyst
        finds
Poison A bobby peals at the front door
our mum stays mum our dad knows nowt e says
'n in Nigeria aa get a letter
Dear John don't ever think aa'd kill mysel -
aa don't know wot to think things are that bad.

X.

IN TEESSIDE Dad's well-liked well-known well-
        placed
but can't or won't get work wen e retires
tries Manchester then London 'n squats there
clerkin for a small business In is Lodge
e bears the offices in their due rota
Dad pays a visit ome 'N Mother dies

DEAR JOHN your mothers dead in ospital
We were quite tender that last night at ome -

Dad brings is Deepdale bits and pieces back
'n scraps Mum's relics photos papers books
except the crumpled pound notes in odd corners
A pippin slowly witherin 'n sweetenin

POUNCIN to burn me little silhouette
a' Mother aa find pressed in the big book
of the Great Exhibition with engravins
a farm sale trophy f'm deep in the Dales
Dad joins the MCC taks trips to Lords
'n visits Duncan's family at Xmas

XI.

'N SUMMERTIME Like Duncan's courtin leads im
to Hull 'n Mary 'n a stalwart marriage
Mother declines to attend so so does Dad
'n aa'm best man Our parents greet the pair
at the train's Darlo call Duncan's still trainin
wen e'n Mary ave a daughter Rosemary

GUILDFORD 'n Dereham Maidenhead 'n Camborne
Cardiff 'n back to Humberside yer grandparents
can tell you all there is to know 'n more
most likely Yer dad Andy's their first son
'n then Robin 'n Wendy They're all four
our Dad's deepest delight Ro first of all

MOTHER taks agin Mary f'm the first
wet nappies part brass rags Later on Andy
'n Ro pay visits 'n wee Robin calls
wi' Duncan At long range they correspond
generations apart as aa sustain
Mother's grass-widow'ood wiles breakdown nudges

XII.

AA TAK a post in Ethiopia
'n ave Dad's numbin news Oo really cares
now Jo'burg 'n another university
Adelaide seven runways off by air
brings me the title role in Osborne's Luther
at the Jesuit College 'n the breakdown

SO AA'M COMPANY for Dad 'n company
for younger mates as don't get on wi' dads
else loses em 'N most a' all for Michael
the maimed deaf 'airdresser me demon-angel
since self-slain like me family favourite Andy
A bean-pole bard's the newest foster-son

FRESH BREAKDOWNS force retirement in me forties
'n aa omes in on verse too bent on writin
to chivvy publishers as well as words
Numbers come easier now than prose 5,000
poems in the marshallin yards as many more
seedlins needlin towards the light to come

XIII.

GAUGE PARENTS by their brats 'n ours score igh
Their parents failed each other 'n emsels
Ours aimed too igh The sky's a dodgy target
Livin for us livin to see us grow
appy 'n grateful carryin their banners
our lives a testimony to their love

XIV.

MY DEAR GREAT-NIECE dear Fae Boudicca
    Deepdale
POSTSCRIPT Throughout for Deepdale read yer own
true name (Poets entered in the Cleveland Games
or other races sprint or middle-distance
or Marathon must run in ski-masks now
for fear we bolt or drug or lame the judges

YET we must figure to renew the race)
This is for you yer cousins 'n yer seed
Yer father's gone yer mother's line's sealed off
kindly fm kinhood's tree Here's me own lineage
one arf a' yours So for yer father's sake
Fae keep our memories green as yer keep 'is ::

1990

Next Poem